Where Did They Go?
Dragons flew over castles.
Dragons flew over clouds.
Dragons gathered in flocks in the sky.
Dragons flew in graceful crowds.
I've searched the sky for hours.
I've searched the sky,
 for a lifetime it seems.
I've looked for the wisp of a tail or scale.
I've searched my mind —
 were they only in dreams?
Where did they fly off to?
Where did they decide to land?
Where on earth — or was it beyond?
Where did they go? I don't understand.

Leslie Tryon

Dragon
Mythical beast
Watches a passing knight
Silent death dropping from the sky
Battle

J.E. Moore

Let's Learn About Dragons

Read About Dragons

Adam Draws Himself a Dragon by Irina Korschunow; Harper & Row, 1978 (Grades 2-3)

The Dragon Kite by Nancy Luenn; Harcourt Brace Jovanovich, 1982 (Grades 3-4)

The Dragon Nanny by C. L. B. Martin; Macmillan, 1989 (Grades 2-3)

Everyone Knows What a Dragon Looks Like by Judy Williams; Four Winds, 1976 (Grades 3-4)

Eyes of the Dragon by Margaret Leaf; Lothrop, 1987 (Grades 2-4)

The Knight and the Dragon by Tomie de Paola; Putnam, 1980 (Grades 2-3)

The Knight, the Princess, and the Dragon by Helen Craig; Knopf, 1985 (Grade 2)

The Loathsome Dragon by David Wiesner and Kim Kahng; G.P. Putnam's Sons, 1987 (Grades 2-4)

My Father's Dragon by Ruth Gannett; Random, 1948 (Grades 2-3)

The Reluctant Dragon by Kenneth Grahame; Holiday, 1938 (Grades 3-4)

Saint George and the Dragon by Margaret Hodges; Little, 1984 (Grade 4)

The Truth About Dragons by Rhoda Blumberg; Four Winds Press, 1980 (Grades 2-4). This book is out of print right now, but can probably be found in your school or public library.

Poems About Dragons

The Tale of Custard the Dragon by Ogden Nash
The Gold-Tinted Dragon by Karla Kuskin
A Modern Dragon by Rowena Bennett
The Toaster by William Jay Smith
Dragon Smoke by Lillian Moore

Note: This activity may be done as a whole class brainstorming session or in cooperative-learning groups. Combine all information to create a large chart to leave up in the class throughout the unit of study. Update the chart as the unit progresses.

Before We Begin

What we know about dragons.	What we want to learn about dragons.

A Dragon Book

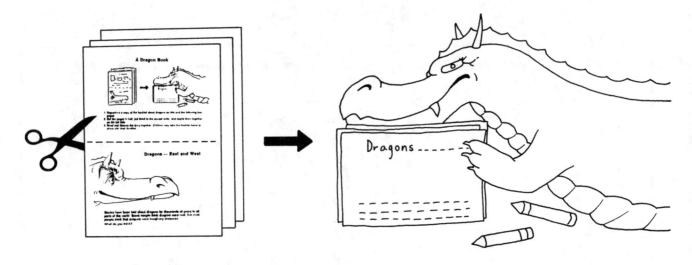

1. Reproduce a copy of the booklet about dragons on this and the following two pages.
2. Cut the pages in half, put them in the correct order, and staple them together on the left side.
3. Read and discuss the story together. Children may take the booklet home to share with their families.

Dragons — East and West

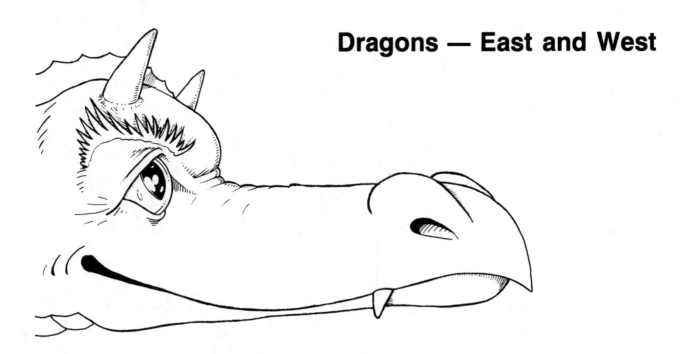

Stories have been told about dragons for thousands of years in all parts of the world. Some people think dragons were real, but most people think that dragons were imaginary creatures.

What do you think?

 Dragons

In the western countries, people usually thought that dragons were fearful and dangerous beasts. They were afraid a huge dragon might fly down from the sky and burn their homes and eat their children.

Draw a fierce dragon flying in the sky.

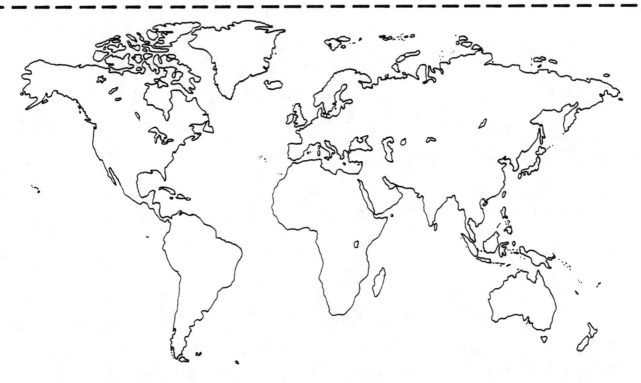

In eastern countries such as China and Japan, people usually thought that dragons were friendly, wise and helpful. They felt that dragons controlled the weather and could provide wealth and good fortune.

Find China and Japan on the map.

 Dragons

Western dragons are often drawn as huge, scaly beasts with wings, sharp claws, and a barbed tail. They breathe fire or poison gases. The dragon might have a head like a lion or an eagle or a body like a snake. Some dragons even had more than one head.

Can you name the parts of this dragon?

- -

Eastern dragons are drawn in many different ways. Some are as tiny as an insect while others are enormous. They could change appearance and some could become invisible. Some had wings and some did not. In China, ordinary dragons had four claws, while royal dragons had five claws. In Japan, the dragons had three claws.

Circle the Japanese dragon and underline the royal Chinese dragon.

   Dragons

Note: Children are to decide if the statement is true about western dragons, eastern dragons, both types, or none.

Think About It

	Western Dragons	Eastern Dragons	Both	None
1. These dragons could change their form.				
2. These dragons were fierce and evil.				
3. Some of these dragons lived on the moon.				
4. These dragons brought good fortune.				
5. These dragons had wings covered with feathers.				
6. These dragons fought with knights in armor.				
7. These dragons could become invisible.				
8. People thought these dragons controlled the weather.				
9. These dragons are still living in South American jungles.				
10. These dragons often destroyed villages.				
11. These dragons had scaly bodies.				
12. These dragons liked to eat people.				

Dragons

Dragon Search

You may use the encyclopedia, the dictionary, or library books to find the answers to these questions.

1. What type of creature is a dragon?

_____

_____

2. How are western dragons and eastern dragons different?

_____

_____

3. Can you name two of the famous dragon slayers?

_____

_____

4. Which constellation is named for a dragon?

_____

_____

5. In which Chinese celebration is a dragon part of a parade?

_____

_____

6. Which type of dragons were believed to control the weather?

_____

_____

Write a question of your own. Challenge another group to find the answer.

We ask this question: _____

_____

The other group (was — was not) able to find the answer.

Animal Families
Where Would a Dragon Belong?

Read these descriptions of animal families. Where do you think a dragon would fit best?

Mammal

fur or hair on body
babies born alive
babies fed milk from
 mother's body
warm-blooded
breathe air with lungs

Birds

body covered with feathers
lay eggs with hard-shells
wings
warm-blooded
beak

Reptile

covered with scales or plates
skin is rough and dry
most lay eggs
cold-blooded
breathe air with lungs

Amphibians

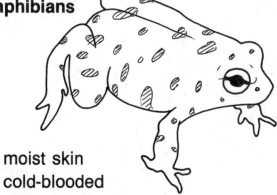

moist skin
cold-blooded
most lay eggs in water
live on land as adults
hatch from jelly-covered eggs

A dragon could be a part of the _____ family for these reasons:

_____

_____

_____

_____

Note: Begin Venn diagrams as a whole-group activity until children are comfortable making comparisons in this way.

Dragon and Dinosaur
Compare and Contrast

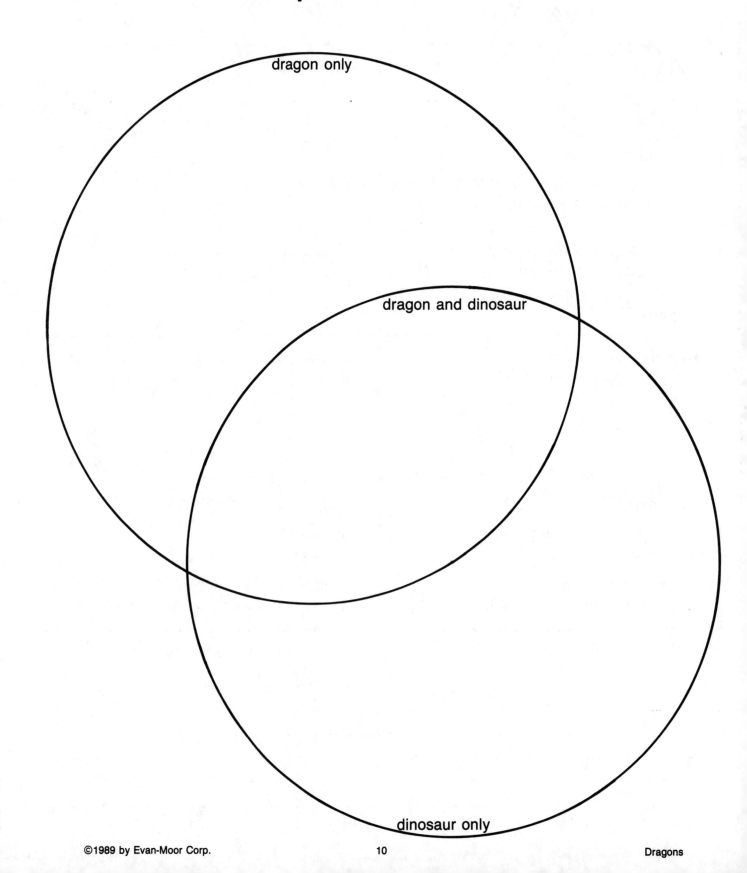

Note: Use this activity sheet to practice distinguishing between real and imaginary animals. You may want to do it orally with younger students.

Real or Make-Believe?

Read about the animal. If it is a real animal, circle it. If it is an imaginary animal, cross it out.

This kitten likes to play with a rubber mouse. He chases his brothers around the back yard.

This gigantic blue whale is the largest animal that ever lived.

The unicorn has a horn right in the middle of its forehead.

This gigantic bird can pick a ship up out of the ocean and carry it away in its claws.

This little spider could weave messages in her web.

This large ape climbed the Empire State Building.

This little insect collects pollen from flowers and makes honey for us to eat.

This monkey went out to get a job. He made a mess of every job he tried.

This black and white bird can't fly, but he is a great swimmer.

This dinosaur ate New York City.

Dragons

What Do You Think?
Which is hotter? Why?

A desert or a dragon's tongue? _____

_____

The inside of a toaster or a dragon's mouth? _____

_____

Old Faithful or a dragon's breath? _____

_____

Scalding steam or a dragon's tears? _____

_____

Think About Dragons
Is a dragon more like...Why?

a lizard or a snake? _____

_____

a fairy tale or a legend? _____

_____

a bird or a bat? _____

_____

a volcano or an oven? _____

_____

Note: These can be done orally or in written form. They may be done by the whole class, in cooperative-learning groups, or put on cards for a free-time center activity.

What would it be like?

What would a dragon's _____ be like?

tears _____

_____

laugh _____

_____

song _____

_____

breath _____

_____

What does it feel like to be a dragon?

What would _____ a dragon?

anger _____

_____

amuse _____

_____

embarrass _____

_____

frighten _____

_____

A Drove of Dragons

There are many words used to describe groups of animals. See how many of these you know. See if someone else in the class can help you with the ones you do not know. Work together to find the answers that no one knows.

1. A _____ of geese

2. A _____ of whales

3. A _____ of bees

4. A _____ of fish

5. A _____ of quail

6. A _____ of elephants

7. A _____ of giraffes

8. A _____ of wolves

9. A _____ of lions

10. A _____ of kangaroos

11. A _____ of people

Use Your Imagination
Make up a character (real or imaginary) for each of these groups:

A dribble of _____

A shout of _____

A whoosh of _____

 Dragons

Note: Children work in pairs. One portrays the dragon, the other conducts the interview. With younger children, select a dragon and have the rest of the class conduct the interview as an oral activity.

A Dragon Interview

What is your name?

Where were you born?

Where do you live now?

Tell about your childhood.

How did you learn to fly?

What makes you sad?

What makes you happy?

Other questions I would ask...

Note: This activity is designed to help children create more interesting sentences. You may want to use the following page for sentence writing.

A dragon flew.

1. Brainstorm — Fill in one category at a time beginning with describing words. List the children's suggestions on the chalkboard or a chart. (Older children may want to use a dictionary at this point to find more challenging words.)

2. Oral Sentences — Allow time for children to create many oral sentences using the words and phrases on the chalkboard.

3. Write — Have the children select one word or phrase from each column to create interesting sentences.

	describing words	who or what	did what?	where?	when?

Add these words and phrases to increase vocabulary and to develop new concepts.

describing words:

1. terrible
2. fierce
3. unique
4. mythical

did what?

1. vanished
2. attacked the village
3. changed shape
4. escaped

where?

1. behind the clouds
2. at the edge of an abyss
3. deep in the forest
4. into the stormy night

when?

1. long, long ago
2. just before dawn
3. in ancient times
4. as the sun set

 Dragons

A Dragon

How many sentences did you write? _____
Illustrate one sentence on the back of this paper.

Note: Each child will need a copy of the worksheet on the following page.

A Class Flip Book

Here is another way to practice creative sentence writing.

1. Each child needs a worksheet.

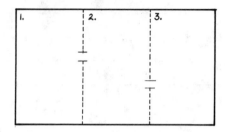

2. Write:

Box 1 — Child names and describes the subject.
Example: A huge, scaly dragon

Box 2 — Child tells what action is taking place.
Example: flew

Box 3 — Child tells where and when the action occurred.
Example: into the clouds as the sun set.

3. Illustrate:

Child creates a picture that matches the description. Neck and tail must meet the cross lines so that all pages will match when the book is put together.

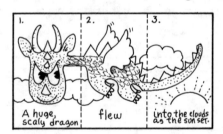

4. Put the book together:

Staple the pages together with a cover. Cut the pages apart on the dotted lines. Now each section can be turned independently to create humorous new pictures and sentences.

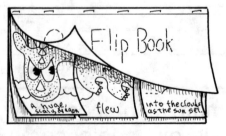

Older students may want more writing space. This can be provided by gluing or taping writing paper to the bottom of the original worksheet.

2.

3.

Imagine a Dragon

Does your dragon have...

scales? _____

wings? _____

claws? how many? _____

What is your dragon's name? _____

Describe your dragon:

length _____

weight _____

body covering _____

color _____

age _____

Get a sheet of paper. Write a paragraph describing the special talents and characteristics of your dragon.

Dragons

Dragon Graphs

Use the information from "Imagine a Dragon" activity sheets to create a graph about dragons. You can graph information such as height, weight, age, type of body covering, wings or wingless, etc.

EXAMPLE:

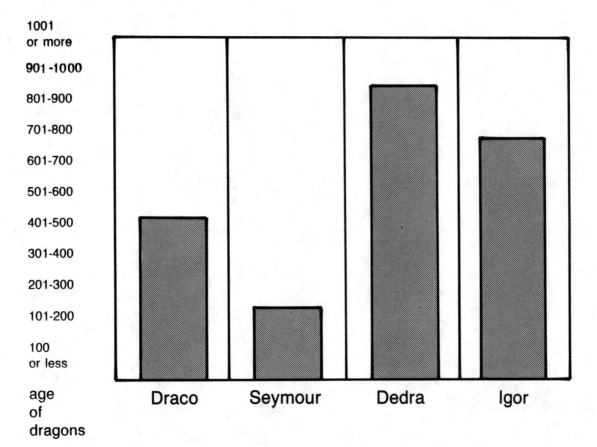

Ask questions such as:
(Select questions suitable for the age and ability of your students.)

1. Which dragon is the oldest?

2. Which dragon is the youngest?

3. Are any of the dragons in the same age range?

4. How many dragons are between 301 and 400 years old?

5. Are more dragons older than 500 or younger than 500?

Dot-to-Dot Dragon

Start at 1.

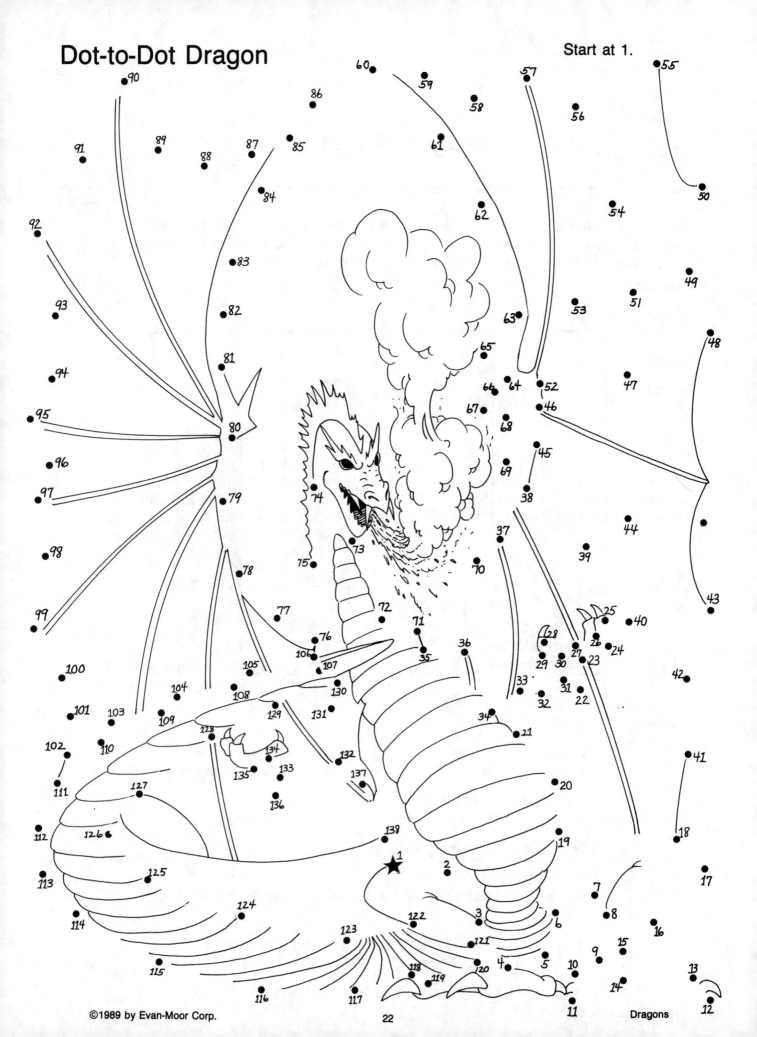

22

Dragons

Note: Use the problems which are suitable for the age and ability of your students. Have them help make up more story problems using dragons as a theme.

Dragon Story Problems

The dragon flew 24 miles before noon. He flew 18 miles after noon. How far did he fly that day?

With each blast from his nostrils, the dragon scorched whatever it hit. Yesterday he burned 27 pine trees, 15 hay stacks and 7 barns. How many things did he set fire in all?

To win his knighthood, Cedric the page was charged with returning to the royal kitchen with 400 kilograms of dragon eggs. If one dragon egg weighs 8 kilograms, how many eggs must Cedric find?

48 knights rode out to fight a dragon. 32 knights came back to the castle. How many knights did the dragon kill?

The old dragon had a huge treasure. He planned to divide it among his three children. He kept the treasure in 15 chests. How many chests will each dragon child get?

Org the dragon has an incredible sweet tooth. During his last raid on the village bakery, he consumed 3 dozen jelly doughnuts, 16 loaves of raisin bread weighing 24 ounces each, and 42 cherry pies. How many pastries did Org devour?

Note: Discuss possible "life-cycle" stages for a dragon. Older students can create their own written description of the cycle.

A Dragon Life Cycle

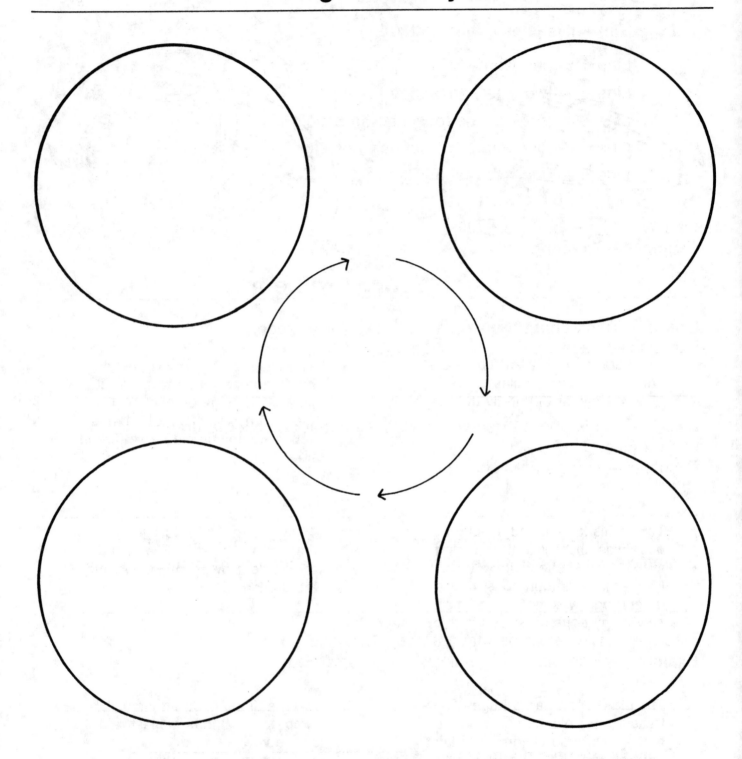

Dragons hatch from eggs. They grow larger each day. Gradually their wings begin to grow. When the wings are big and strong the young dragon begins to learn to fly. The young dragon also begins to learn to breathe fire. Adult females lay eggs, and the cycle begins again.

24   Dragons

Note: Spend some time brainstorming about dragons (in each category) before children begin writing their cinquain.

Create a Dragon Poem — Cinquain

Cinquain — five lines in this pattern:

    Line 1 — one word (title)

    Line 2 — two words (describe the title)

    Line 3 — three words (describe an action)

    Line 4 — four words (describe a feeling)

    Line 5 — one word (about the title)

Line 1 — Pick a one word title
Example — Dragon

_____

Line 2 — Think about two words that describe a dragon.
Example — huge, scaly   flaming nostrils

_____

Line 3 — Think about three words that tell about an action a dragon might make.
Example — follows a knight   dives to earth

_____

Line 4 — Think about four words that tell how the dragon might feel.
Example — bravely protects its home   eager for its dinner

_____

Line 5 — Think of words that tell about dragons.
Example — warrior   hungry   mythical

_____

Copy your whole poem on a clean sheet of paper.

Dragon
Huge, scaly
Ready to fight
Bravely protects its home
Warrior

Note: Write a descriptive paragraph or original poem on the center section of the dragon.

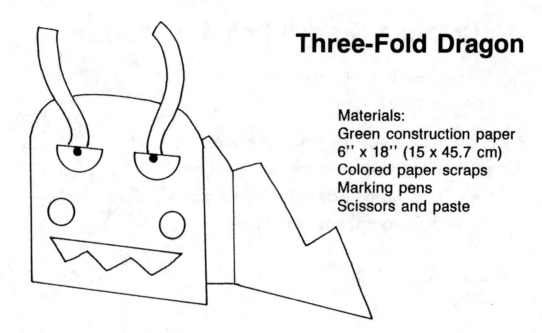

Three-Fold Dragon

Materials:
Green construction paper
6'' x 18'' (15 x 45.7 cm)
Colored paper scraps
Marking pens
Scissors and paste

Steps to follow:

1. Fold a 6'' x 18'' paper in thirds.

2. Round off the top corners of section 1. Zig-zag cut the top edges of sections 2 and 3.

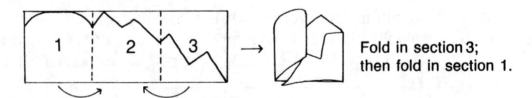

Fold in section 3; then fold in section 1.

3. Let imaginations soar in creating a marvelous dragon face on section 1. Use a combination of marking pens or crayons and colored paper scraps.

4. Write or glue in your message on the middle section.

Dragons

Pick A Story

Establish a creative writing center using the next three pages.

• Sentence Strips

1. Copy each page on a different color paper.
2. Laminate the pages if possible.
3. Cut the strips apart and place in the castle card holder.

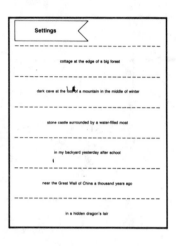

Characters
fierce, flying dragon   brave knight   beautiful princess
kind dragon   small boy   magic box
huge three-headed dragon   clumsy knight   smart maiden
an invisible dragon   wise old man   angry king
tiny dragon   pet cat   curious child
unusual dragon   old woman   hunter

Settings
cottage at the edge of a big forest
dark cave at the foot of a mountain in the middle of winter
stone castle surrounded by a water-filled moat
in my backyard yesterday after school
near the Great Wall of China a thousand years ago
in a hidden dragon's lair

Situations
a search for dragon's treasure
someone lost who is trying to find the way home
a wounded dragon seeking...help, vengeance, or a magic potion
someone has been taken by a dragon and must be rescued
a strange door has been opened between the past and the present time
a misunderstanding causes trouble

• Castle Card Holder

1. Reproduce the turret pattern on the inside back cover.
2. Staple a paper pocket on the bottom of each turret to hold the sentence strips.
3. Cut notches in construction paper (8'' X 18'') (20.5 X 45.7 cm) to create the castle walls.
4. Pin all parts to the bulletin board.

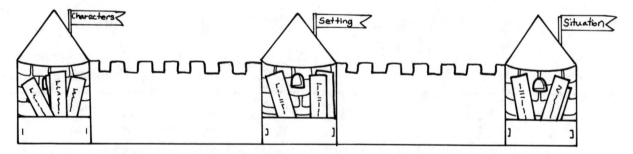

3. Children select one strip of each color. They create original stories using the characters, setting, and situation they have drawn.

Dragons

Characters

fierce, flying dragon   brave knight   beautiful princess

kind dragon   small boy   magic box

huge three-headed dragon   clumsy knight   smart maiden

an invisible dragon   wise old man   angry king

tiny dragon   pet cat   curious child

unusual dragon   old woman   hunter

Settings

cottage at the edge of a big forest

dark cave at the foot of a mountain in the middle of winter

stone castle surrounded by a water-filled moat

in my backyard yesterday after school

near the Great Wall of China a thousand years ago

in a hidden dragon's lair

Situations

a search for dragon's treasure

someone lost who is trying to find the way home

a wounded dragon seeking...help, vengeance, or a magic potion

someone has been taken by a dragon and must be rescued

a strange door has opened between the past and the present time

a misunderstanding causes trouble

Note: Guide your students through the steps below to create a pop-up dragon to use as a cover for original dragon stories. You may need to cut the paper to size for second graders.

A Dragon Pop-Up Book

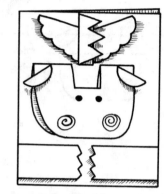

Materials: Construction paper
        green 12" X 18" (30.5 X 45.7 cm)
           9" X 12" (22.9 X 30.5 cm)
       scraps in many colors
       Ruler
       Scissors
       Glue

Steps to follow:

1. Cut the paper as shown below.

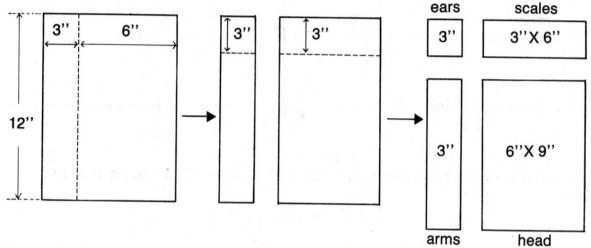

2. Head — Follow the steps shown below.

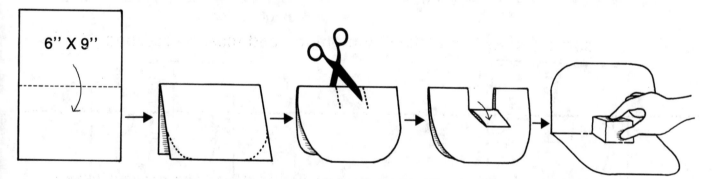

3. Ears, Arms, Scales — Follow the steps shown below.

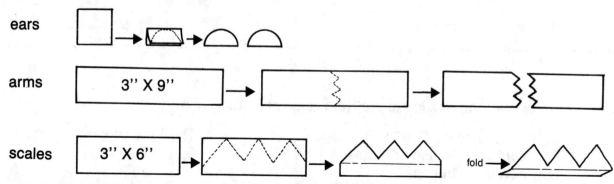

Dragons

4. Complete the head by adding horns and nostrils made from colorful scraps of paper.

Add eyes with crayon.

5. Cut "flames" from red and yellow scraps. Put paste on the top of the pop-up tab and paste flames in place.

Assemble the cover — Follow the steps shown below.

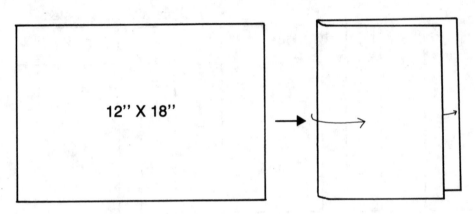

12" X 18"

Fold the cover.

Paste the dragon pieces to the cover.

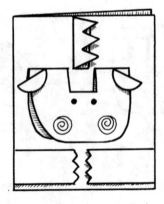

Optional — Add wings cut from a bright color.

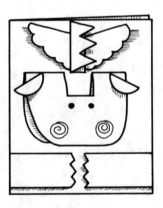

Here are some sample titles to motivate reluctant writers:

1. How to Breathe Fire by D. Dragon
2. Knight and Dragon...Friends or Foes?
3. If I Were a Dragon
4. The Last Dragon on Earth
5. Space Dragons

Note: You will need to reproduce the patterns on the following page to accompany this lesson.

Conversations With a Dragon

Discussion:
You will need to spend some time talking about possible conversations that could occur between a dragon and any of the other characters. Record the students' ideas on the chalkboard or a chart for future reference.

Prepare your paper:

Simple Conversation — Each child needs a 12" X 18" sheet of construction paper and a copy of the patterns on the following page.

1. Color and cut out a dragon and one other character. Paste them to the construction paper.

2. Draw speech "bubbles" with black crayon or marking pen. (Or use bubbles cut from lined writing paper.)

3. Draw a background.

4. Write the conversation inside the speech bubbles.

Cartoon Story — Each child will need a 12" X 18" or larger sheet of construction or butcher paper and one or more copies of the patterns on the following page.

1. Make an outline of the story plot. Keep it simple! Plan what will happen in each box.

2. Select the characters to be used (or draw your own). Color and cut out the characters.

3. Fold your paper into four, six, or eight parts depending on the length of your story. Paste the characters in the boxes. Draw in the speech bubbles. Add background to your pictures.

4. Write the dialogue in the bubbles.

Clip-Art Patterns

Dragons

Dragon Masks

Create masks from brown paper bags and construction paper scraps.

Create masks from a sheet of paper and construction paper scraps.

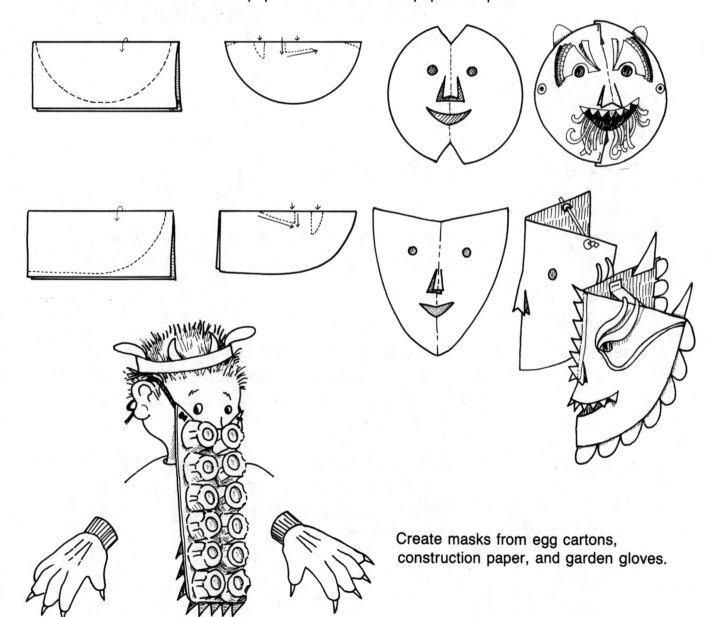

Create masks from egg cartons,
construction paper, and garden gloves.

 Dragons

Note: You may want to have children make one of the masks on the preceding page to wear as they present this short play.

Those Bad, Braggin' Dragons

The dragons are trying out for the starring role in a video. The director auditions them at the same time.

Character	Dialogue
Director	Alright, dragons, would you like to tell me a little about yourselves? I'm looking for a real talent to star in my new video, "Bad Dragons."
Mean Dean	I'm Mean Dean a fire breathin' machine.
Torchy Sadie	I'm Torchy Sadie the dragon lady.
Director	Tell me Dean, and Sadie too, exactly what you two would do if I said "ACTION — it's your cue"?
Mean Dean	I'd stoke up all my fires by taking a giant breath. I'd open my jaws and scorch my teeth. I'd scare you half to death.
Torchy Sadie	I'd sing up and down a scale, such a shrill and unearthly sound, that glass would break and walls would fall, and cracks would open up in the ground.

Dragons

Mean Dean	(Feeling the spirit of competition, he rises to his feet and continues.) I'd flap my wings, breathe fire and roar. I'd lift off the ground and take flight. I'd spread my wings and cover the sun, making it blacker than the darkest night.
Torchy Sadie	(She gets up at this point too.) I'd sing a note that would loosen my scales. They'd fall to the ground in a pile. They'd all sprout legs and a voice like mine, screeching and marching, single file.
Director	I love it! I love it! You're both just great! This is my lucky day. It must be fate. I'll take you both. You're really first rate. We'll tape in the a. m. Your call is at eight.

Draw a Dragon

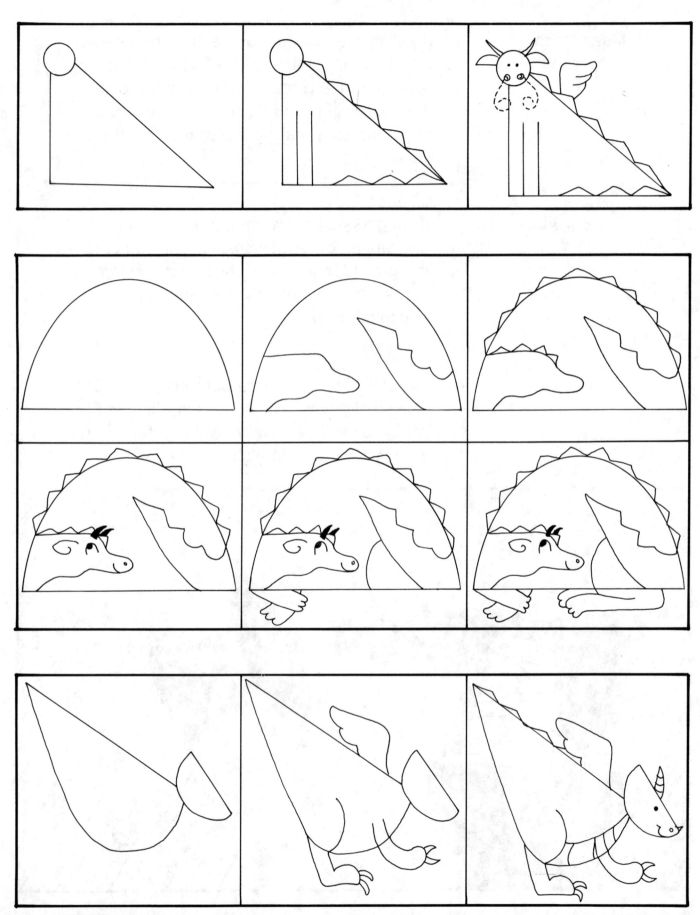

Dragons

Note: Younger students will need guidance to successfully complete this activity.

Create
Three-Dimensional Dragons

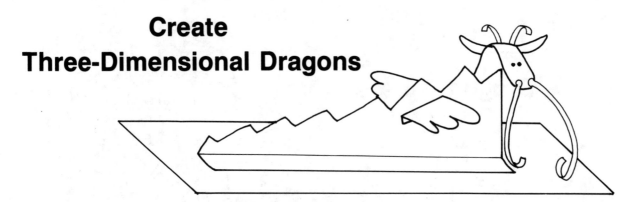

Materials:

> Green and brown construction paper 12" X 18" (30.5 X 45.7 cm)
> A box of scraps in assorted colors
> Crayons or marking pens
> Scissors and glue.

> The dragon on this page is only an example of what you can make.
> Use your imagination to create a dragon of your own.
> Decide what you want your dragon to look like.
>> fierce or funny?
>> large or small?
>> wings or no wings?

Steps to follow:

1. Cut the dragon's body out of the large green paper. Make a fold along the bottom. Put glue along this fold. Glue the dragon's body to the brown paper.

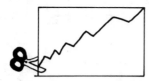 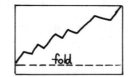 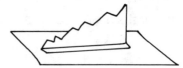

2. Cut a head from the green scraps you have left. Add eyes with crayons or marking pens.

   Use colored scraps to add other features (horns, ears, fire coming out of mouth).

   Glue features to the head. Glue the head to the body.

3. Use colored scraps if you want to add wings to your dragon.

Note: This is a group activity. You will need a large area to display the dragon when it is complete.

A Dragon Mural

Head:
Select a group of children to design a head for the dragon.
It is made from a large brown paper bag and paper scraps.
Make colored paper, aluminum foil, tissue paper, and colored cellophane available for a magnificent finished product.

Body:
Each student designs one 12" X 18" (30.5 X 45.7 cm) scale.

Create a "scaly" pattern on the paper with black crayon or marking pen.

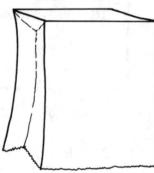

round the corners

Feet and Wings:
Add colorful claws to the feet.
Select someone to design and make tissue paper wings.

Putting the mural together:
Pin the head to the bulletin board.
Arrange the scales in a pleasing manner.
Add the wings.

Dragons

Note: These activities may be done orally or in written form. They may be done by individual students, in co-operative-learning groups, or as whole-class experiences.

Open-Ended Activities to Use With Books About Dragons

Re-tell the story:

- in outline form
- in the "5 Ws" form (who, did what, where, when, why)
- in paragraph form using your own words
- as a short play, puppet show, radio show, etc.
- in a comic book format
- setting it in a new location or time period

Describe:

- a character from the story
- a setting or location important to the story
- a feeling or mood
- one particular event

Find examples of:

- cause and effect
- fact or fiction
- figures of speech
- descriptive language

Share the book with others:

- give a book talk
- write a book review
- create an advertisement
- make a new book cover

Compare and contrast:

- characters within the story
- two books with a similar theme
- two books by the same author or illustrator

My Father's Dragon
by Ruth Stiles Gannett

Elmer cleverly used the items in his knapsack to escape from the wild animals. Imagine yourself in a dangerous situation in a strange, wild place. You must get across a wide river and up a high mountain. There are angry hippos in the river and baboons in the woods on the side of the mountain.

What are you carrying with you that might be helpful?

_____

_____

_____

How would you get across the river full of angry hippos?

_____

_____

_____

How would you get up the mountain past the baboons?

_____

_____

_____

What would you do as soon as you reached safety?

_____

_____

_____

Note: Read Adam Draws Himself a Dragon by Irina Korschunow to your students. (Older students may want to read it for themselves.)

Adam Draws Himself a Dragon

by Irina Koschunow

The dragons in this story have three heads each and each head blows out a different color of fire. Make your own three-headed dragon.

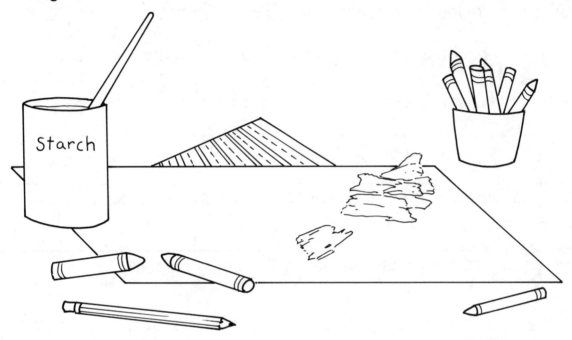

1. Get a large sheet of drawing paper. Draw a three-headed dragon.

2. Take pieces of red, yellow, and blue tissue paper. Tear the tissue paper into small pieces.
   Brush liquid starch where you want you "fire" to go. Lay the pieces of tissue paper on the starch. Brush over the tissue paper with more starch. Let your picture dry completely.

3. Draw a background for you dragon picture. Try to make the picture tell a story.

4. Get a sheet of writing paper. Describe your dragon and explain what it can do.

 Dragons

Note: Read Saint George and the Dragon by Margaret Hodges to your students. (This book is most appropriate for older students.) They will need to hear the description on page 15 several times before doing this drawing activity.

Saint George and the Dragon

by Margaret Hodges

The illustrator has taken the author's descriptions and created her version of the mighty dragon in this story. Listen carefully as your teacher reads the description of the dragon. (You may need to hear it more than one time.) You may want to make some notes as you listen to help you remember when you begin to draw.

1. Think about the words the author uses to describe the dragon.
   Example: vast, scales of brass, speckled

_____

_____

2. Think about where the dragon is and what it is doing.
   Example: up on its hind legs

_____

_____

3. Think about the feeling you get as you hear the words. You will want your picture to have the same feeling.

_____

_____

4. Make some rough sketches of the dragon on scratch paper. This will give you a chance to try out your ideas.

5. Now get a sheet of paper and draw your own version of what the dragon should look like. Finish the picture by adding an interesting background.

Now look at your illustration as the teacher (or yourself) reads the page again. Does it show what the author has described? Is there anything you would change? Compare your version with those of other children in your class to see how the pictures are alike and how they are different.

       Dragons

Note: The next three pages contain blank dragon forms that can be used in many different ways across the curriculum.

Using Dragon Activity Sheet Patterns

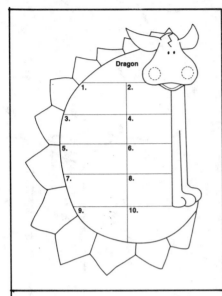

Page 46

- vocabulary lists of dragon words
- spelling words appropriate to the dragon unit
- words for a dictionary search activity
- homework assignments for a week
- language challenges

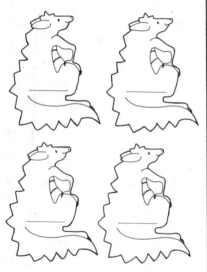

Page 47

- a math problem in each small dragon
  computation
  counting challenges
  word problems
- riddles
- matching activities
- name tags or labels for folders/reports

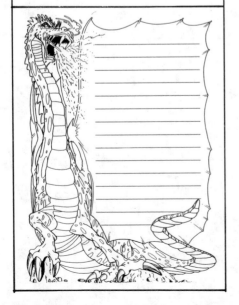

Page 48

- write descriptive paragraphs or original poems
- handwriting practice
- cover art for a report or storybook
- list dragon books read during the unit

Dragons

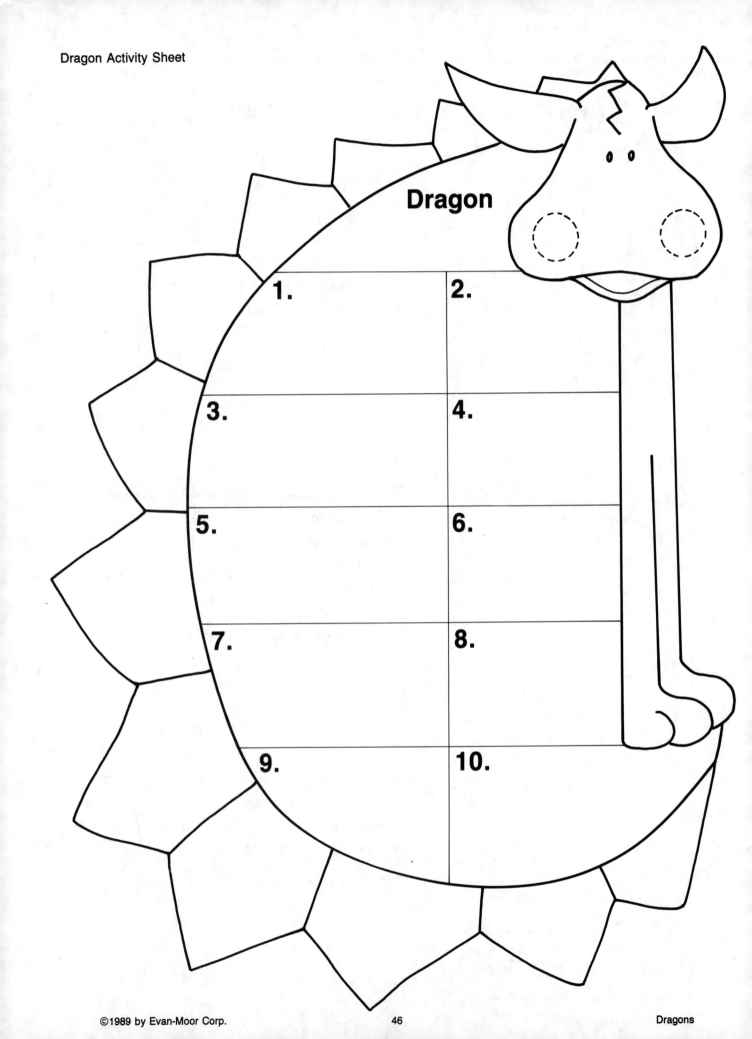

Dragon

1.

2.

3.

4.

5.

6.

7.

8.

9.

10.

Dragons

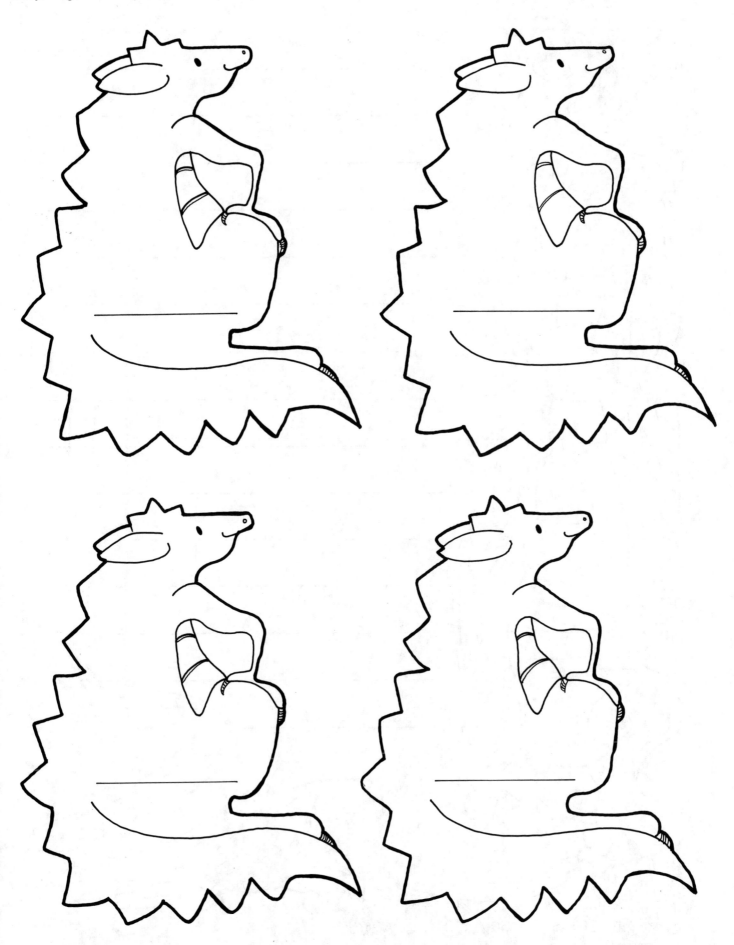

Dragons

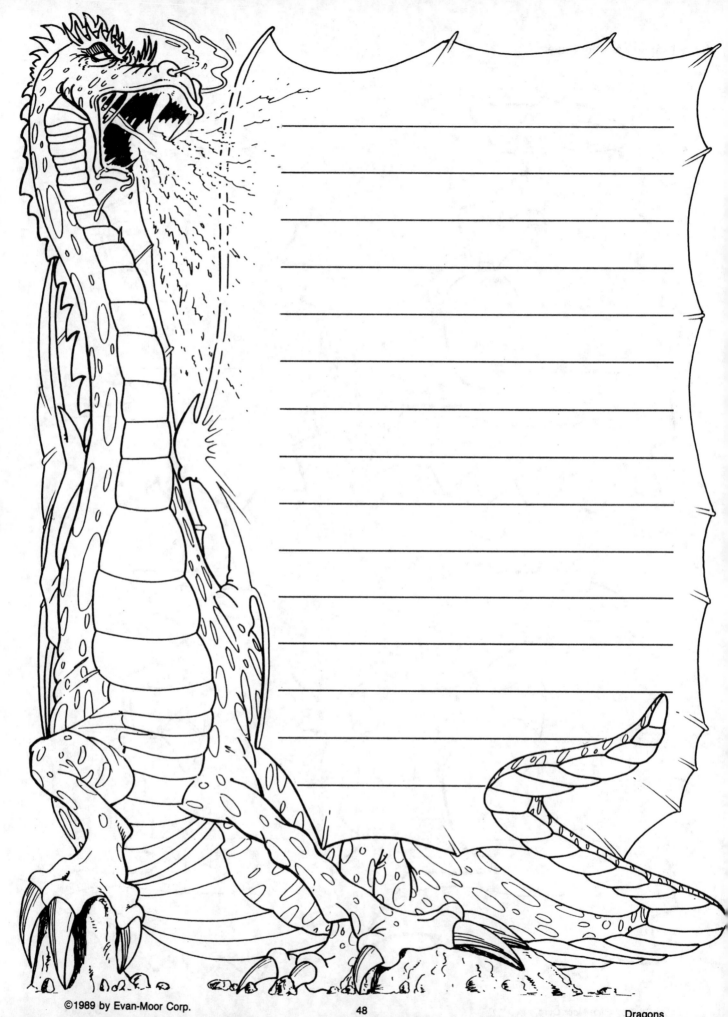

Dragons